Motorcycle Journeys

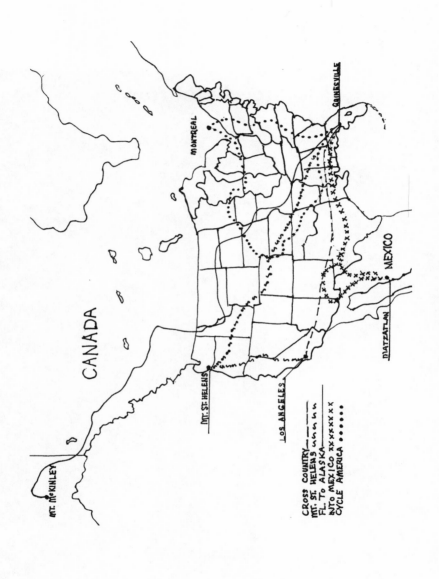

CANADA

MT. McKINLEY

MT. ST. HELENS

LOS ANGELES

MONTREAL

QUINESVILLE

MEXICO

MAZATLAN

CROSS COUNTRY ————
MT. ST. HELENS ∿∿∿∿
FL. TO ALASKA ——————
INTO MEXICO xxxxxxxx
CYCLE AMERICA ••••••

Motorcycle Journeys

Kay McGary

VANTAGE PRESS
New York

FIRST EDITION

Copyright © 2005 by Kay McGary

Published by Vantage Press, Inc.
419 Park Ave. South, New York, NY 10016

Manufactured in the United States of America
ISBN: 0-533-15186-4

Library of Congress Catalog Card No.: 2005901629

0 9 8 7 6 5 4 3 2 1

To Scott

Contents

1

Cross Country

Waiting for the light to change at an intersection in Lake City, Florida, I looked up to see a big, burly man grinning down at me from the cab of his truck. I lifted the shield of my helmet and smiled back. "Hi, Big 18-Wheeler," I said.

"Hi, Little Honda," he returned. He chuckled as he asked, "Are you left over from the old *Laugh In Show?*"

Dressed in my bright yellow rain slicker, I probably looked just like those characters on *Laugh In* who were always dodging a bucket of water. I began to laugh. The trucker and I had communicated. We sat through the next light and talked.

My new friend said he would tell all his CB buddies to watch out for "Little Honda" along the way. I thanked him and as he pulled away, I noticed that his rear plates were from California.

From there on, every truck that passed me either honked or waved. I'm not sure they were all CB buddies of "Big 18-Wheeler" or if it was just my introduction to the fellowship of the open road.

You see, not many women seem inclined, at the age of forty-three, to cross the United States from Gainesville, Florida, to Los Angeles on a Honda 200.

Why was I determined to do it? I was asked just that question in a campground laundry room by a woman from

1

Pennsylvania. My answer wasn't what she obviously expected.

I told her the trip wasn't so much just for myself as it was for all the people I've known, who have touched my life with their own special dreams and hopes, but for various reasons were unable to fulfill them. I pursued my dream; maybe they, too, will find theirs.

I've always wanted to see more of this country and its people. What better way than by motorcycle, camping along the road? For some reason people will talk to you traveling on a motorcycle, but ignore you when you're safely encased in a car. Perhaps it's curiosity . . . perhaps just a tinge of wanting to do what you are doing.

A note to the Gainesville Chamber of Commerce: as I rode through Tallahassee, Florida, taking a side tour through the Florida State University campus, I realized how much planning it took (and is still taking), to make Gainesville and the University of Florida campus so much more convenient and picturesque. I was proud of Gainesville.

From Tallahassee, I followed Interstate 10 to Mobile, Alabama, and got a fair idea of what surfers mean when they "shoot the tube." That's exactly what it felt like, riding through the George Wallace Tunnel outside Mobile. At 50 miles an hour on a motorcycle, you feel totally surrounded by wall and totally vulnerable. It was never like that in a car.

Next came Gulfport, Mississippi, and on to Louisiana. Here I got my first introduction to the snarls and criss-crossings of superhighways. Seemed like a terrible waste of concrete, but I finally wound up in downtown New Orleans.

On the weekend before St. Patrick's Day, the city was jumping. I was bound for the French Quarter, just to say I'd been there, and after an hour of riding down streets lined with bars, taverns and lounges, and jammed with people dancing and singing in the streets, I began to suspect that the pulse of this city beat twice as fast as most others.

For the practical minded, I had reached Louisiana having ridden over 700 miles, at a cost of $12.84 for gas and $12.56 for camping facilities. Not counting the freeze-dried food I carried with me, my total eating costs were just under $8.

I carried a small Peak II camp stove for cooking, a sleeping bag, backpacker's tent, clothing (mostly jeans and sweatshirts), and incidentals, making my total weight of 150 pounds. The biggest problem was keeping such essentials as a rain suit, gloves, camera and an extra sweater for warmth in easily accessible places amid other paraphernalia.

As a pixyish lady in her sixties told me at a stop along the way, "If I were only a little younger, I'd try it."

Next stop, Houston, Texas.

Seems like as soon as I'd left Louisiana and entered Texas, it began to rain. Texas is big, big state. If you don't believe it, try crossing it on a small, small motorcycle.

"Little Honda," and I were in for it. Backed by 55-mile-per-hour winds, the rain had the force of needles. I pulled off and donned more clothing under my rain suit. Back on the bike, where passing drivers shook their heads as they glanced over at me, bent forward against the wind.

When the rain finally let up, I pulled into a rest area to stretch my legs. The park attendant had worked there for thirty-some years, and said most folks who stopped took time to share a few of their on-the-road experiences with him. He'd done some motorcycling as a young man and we swapped a few stories before I went on my way.

A few miles down the road, I stopped to help an elderly lady who couldn't find the hood latch on the foreign car she

3

was driving. Her small grandson watched wide-eyed from the passenger's side as I added oil to the crankcase and waited while she restarted the car.

"Isn't it wonderful what some people are able to do nowadays," the lady said as she thanked me. Her grandson, clad in a T-shirt showing Eval Knieval on his motorcycle, peered over at "Little Honda" with a smile on his face.

After a day in Houston visiting with an old college friend, her husband and family, it was on to San Antonio, where I played the total tourist. I found myself following the old "Mission Trail."

Stopping at Mission Conception, I saw a group of handicapped travelers viewing the area with obvious joy and enthusiasm, traveling in specially-equipped motor homes.

Within the mission, I wandered through corridors and rooms until I reached the sanctuary, where I sat down at the rear of the room and watched people as they entered.

Tears came to my eyes as a blind woman entered on her husband's arm. "You needn't tell me," she whispered to him, "I know I've entered the sanctuary." I, too, felt the peace and reverence of the place, which was reflected upon each person's face as they entered.

Nightfall found me camping just outside Kerrville, Texas. It was beautiful . . . until the temperature started to plummet. As a cold front swept into the area with 25-knot winds, I couldn't get enough clothing on. Wearing long underwear, three sweatshirts, a down vest and blue jeans, boots with two pair of socks, my rain suit and gloves, I attempted to light the small camp stove.

I must have looked like an animated bundle of clothes that someone dropped off for the Goodwill at the picnic table. I finally got the stove lit and heated water for my freeze-dried dinner. Nothing in my whole life tasted so good.

Fellow campers showed me how to put newspapers under my sleeping bag for insulation and warmth. I tucked the camp stove, now turned off, into my tent where it made for a good deal of warmth as it cooled.

To date, I have talked with folks from Kansas, Minnesota, California, Pennsylvania and Alaska, all of whom left me their addresses so that I could stop for a visit if I ever traveled through their town. It's a great country.

In the 1,776 miles "Little Honda" and I have come so far, I have spent $28.59 for camping, and just over $18 for food. "Little Honda" has averaged 70 to 84 miles per gallon. Total maintenance? Chain lubrication daily and 1/3 quart of oil added the third day on the road. Yes—if you're able and willing to tackle things for yourself, I can recommend traveling by motorcycle.

Tomorrow I begin my trek across the desert to California.

At El Paso, I decided to take a little side trip south of the border to visit Ciudad Juarez. I faced a moment of panic when I realized that every sign in the city was in Spanish. Somehow, that hadn't occurred to me on the U.S. side of the border. Fortunately, tourists have been accommodated by adding pictures along with the words.

During my short journey south, I got turned around and headed down a road to lower Mexico. The few words of Spanish that had stuck in my head from high school classes were stretched to the limit, but thanks to the help and concern of the local people, a few hours later I came to a sign that needed no translation . . . "Estados Unitos," followed by a directional arrow.

A short while later, I was able to join the lines of cars at the border crossing, returning from Mexico. While I waited, I decided to take a picture of the customs area. As I stood focusing the camera, I noticed a customs inspector waving his arms madly. I turned to see who he was yelling at and realized it was me! Seems I was violating the Privacy Act with my innocent souvenir photo of the border crossing. Once back in the good ol' U.S.A., however, I vowed never again to complain about governmental red tape or bureaucracy, because where else but in this country are the rights of the individual so diligently protected?

Moving on across the desert, names like John Wesley Hardin, Billy the Kid, Davy Crockett, Saguaro, Mesa, Apache, and Sidewinder became real to me as I visited the historical sites of which they were a part. The highway on which I was traveling followed one of the old trails used by the colonizing Spaniards, the Indians, and the U.S. Cavalry, on the way to Mexico and California. Some of the old Spanish missions and U.S. Cavalry forts built to protect the settlers are still there to see and admire.

The winds start to blow out of the desert in late afternoon and continue until early morning. The dust is as thick as fog on some Florida mornings, so thick that you can't see more than a few feet. I set up my tent in a campground near El Paso. As I crawled in to lie down, the wind was gusting at 40 knots. The tie downs sewed to the tent ripped loose and the only thing holding the tent to the ground was my body inside. What a night!

By early morning I had taken refuge in the campground laundry, where I met a young woman from Canada who was riding a larger motorcycle around the country. She had come 8,000 miles in the past ninety days, traveling from New York to Key West, and was now headed for Las Vegas.

We tried to figure out why Canadians have such an affinity for the American people. She felt it was because Americans always stood up for the underdog, no matter who he might be, that endeared them to our neighbors of the

North. She was the first of many fellow travelers I would meet in the next few days, making the desert miles go faster.

A retired couple from Washington State asked me into their motor home for coffee. They had lived and worked on a farm all their lives without seeing the rest of the country, and now they were doing it at a leisurely pace. "We saved the best for last," they said.

A group of geology students at the University of Arizona swapped tips on trails in the Southwest in exchange for my information on hiking trails and backpacking areas in the east.

Camping at Picacho Peak State Park, I met a twenty-year-old Indian youth who was escorting groups of underprivileged teenagers down the trails and nature paths of that area. His dream was to establish a chain of motels for handicapped travelers at these popular nature areas, so that they, too, could enjoy the wonders of the United States.

Looking down over the desert from the top of Picacho Peak, I felt the wonder of this country, where there were no boundaries—only space and sky—for as far as the eye could see.

When we confine ourselves to a life in the city and limit our horizons to the immediate vicinity, the scope of our existence becomes small. Only when we extend and expand our thoughts and experiences can we truly share. I had come, 3,200 miles in eight-and-a-half days on "Little Honda," and though I didn't set any speed records, the sense of accomplishment was still there.

The trip tested the durability of both bike and rider, but the total cost of gasoline was $42.65. The highest price per gallon that faced me was $1.32 in California. In Mexico, gas was just 65 cents a gallon. Remember those days?

My mileage averaged 75 miles per gallon, and the longest stretch I covered in a single day was 427 miles. What sticks in my mind most "tenderly" was my longest day's ride . . . twelve hours and twenty minutes aboard "Little Honda."

Overnight accommodations in campgrounds ranged from $2.11 to $7.28. The best camping was in state parks, which offered well-informed rangers and marvelous things to do. Food was never a problem, but my preference was for Truck Stops of America, which still offer good food in large amounts at reasonable prices, and where the welcome was always warm. Many towns now have wilderness shops which offer freeze-dried foods for camping.

Would I do it again? At the drop of a hat! I loved every facet of the trip, despite the tired muscles—from the awesome beauty of the terrain to the enduring character of the fellow Americans I met along the way.

Standing on a peak in the middle of the desert, humbly aware of your own insignificance, you come to realize that the words of the song still ring true.

God has, indeed, shed his grace on America!

2

Florida to Mount St. Helens

Every inch of the motorcycle was packed and there wasn't room for another item no matter how small it might happen to be. My many weeks of preparation and planning were at an end and I was about to begin the adventure of seeing and listening to a bit of America on a Honda 400 motorcycle.

The morning was bright and crisp and I had that feeling of "It's great to be alive," when I headed north to Atlanta from my home outside of Gainesville, Florida.

Stopping at rest stops along the way, provides quite an educational and interesting view of America. People who ordinarily would not speak or converse with anyone riding in a car will take time to talk to a lone cycle rider. Whether it be curiosity or concern for a woman traveling alone, I did not know, but nevertheless, I heard many times the thoughts, "You're doing what I always wanted to do" and "I wish I could go with you."

Atlanta offered a great variety of feelings, of business and wonderful hospitality. My stop at Stone Mountain State Park afforded me a chance to hike up the mountain trail and stand atop the world's largest single stone carving.

Listening to the comments of my fellow tourists at the mountain I gained in the knowledge that no matter what your belief or outlook, a work of art is an accomplishment for all of us.

As I left the park, it began to rain and hail and believe me, wearing a helmet was a blessing.

I traveled on through Alabama and part of Mississippi and felt at peace with the beautiful green rolling landscape. I camped at Roosevelt State Park with the temperature dropping to 28 degrees. There were no other tent campers, everyone else was content in the warmth of their RVs. I had an entire shore of the lake to myself and the opportunity to experience the quiet and beauty of a twenty-degree morning. As I crawled from the tent, I was sure the lake would be frozen over, but I was greeted by wild geese in the shallows, racing squirrels and countless birds.

For a small camping fee, I was able to share in a corner of America, preserved in its natural state for everyone to enjoy.

Midmorning found me crossing the Mississippi River, and since one lane of the bridge was blocked off to traffic, I got the chance to take a picture on the state line, right in the center of the bridge. Ahead of me was Louisiana, and reflected in my rearview mirror, Mississippi.

As I turned around for one more shot, I was greeted with a shout of "Hey, what do you think you're doing?" from high above. I glanced up to discover two workers in hardhats, swinging from safety chairs as they worked on the bridge.

My brief explanation of my journey with the cycle brought a story of their own about how they had once crossed the country on Harleys, all while they hung from their safety harnesses and I stood a few feet from whizzing bridge traffic.

Waving good-bye to my two chance acquaintances, I headed west on Interstate 20. Approaching Dallas, I stopped for the night at Tyler State Park. The weather was greatly improved . . . a balmy sixty-eight degrees . . . and the park was nearly filled with friendly travelers.

Since leaving Gainesville, I had traveled 1,071 miles and tomorrow, weather permitting, it was on to the northwest.

The weather surprised me. After leaving Mississippi and Louisiana, it improved steadily. It's nice to be able to shed ten pounds just by storing away your extra sweaters.

The traffic congestion warned me better than any mileage marker that I was nearing Dallas. With the Interstate bypass system, you can get a fair look at the city, but still keep moving . . . if you know where you're going.

If you do misplace yourself, as I did, you may also be lucky enough to meet a state trooper who will let you follow him back to Interstate 35.

As I headed north, I could see the weather changing again. In this flat country, you can watch the weather for many miles ahead. Nothing sneaks up on you.

Certainly, the constant wind blowing across the plains does nothing to dampen spirits in Oklahoma City. If ever there was a modern day "cowboy on the town" spot, that was it. Folks there struck me as robust and hard-working, the kind that politicians like to refer to as "the backbone of America."

Campgrounds are spaced across Oklahoma at convenient intervals, but tenters beware—the wind never stops.

With Interstate 40, I pointed west, heading for Amarillo, Texas. Here the dry desert terrain was a welcome change. So was the sign outside an out-of-way motel near Tucumcari: "American owned, and that makes the difference." It drew me in for the night.

The tiny little lady behind the desk couldn't do enough for me. No long second looks greeted me as I strode through the door in my motorcycle gear. Instead, she informed me that she and her husband, who used to ride cycles before the road was paved had a special room reserved just for cyclers.

"I know just how you feel after riding all day," she said. "Just follow me."

With a good deal of curiosity, I followed her to the room. She opened the door, and there in the corner was an overstuffed rocking chair with a footstool. Heaven! I grinned from ear to ear.

Next morning found me turning north to Denver, Colorado. I began to see hills, followed by mountains, which eventually gave way to snow-capped peaks. What a treat for a Floridian, to see the sun shining on the glistening snow of a mountain.

Once I reached Pueblo, Colorado, the temperature dropped to 35 degrees. Approaching the base of the Rockies, the rolling hills and twisting highways were a motorcyclist's dream. And, you don't have to worry about the motor overheating.

Riding through the countryside, I came across a curious set of signs. The property owner, the signs said, was losing his land because it was needed for an access road. He was going to add a sign a month denouncing the snarls of the government bureaucracy until he got some action on what he called "highway robbery." The four-by-eight-foot signs already stretched for more than a mile.

Where else in the world could an individual protest in this manner? The last sign I rode past said: GOD BLESS YOU, AMERICA, BUT NOT THE GOVERNMENT BUREAUCRATS.

The snow had drifted to ten feet deep in spots as I climbed the Raton Pass through the Rocky Mountains, but the roads were clear. Dozens of cars loaded with ski equipment passed me, headed for the resorts and the last of the winter's snow.

Near Colorado Springs, I passed through the Air Force

Academy property, and saw part of the school within the shadow of Pike's Peak. Denver, billed as the "Mile High City," proved to be one of the most modern and up-to-date cities I've seen in this country, set in spectacular surroundings.

From Florida to Denver and the Rockies was a total of 2,339 miles. To this point, the journey had been uneventful as far as problems with the bike were concerned, but here leaving the Rocky Mountain National Park the chain on the cycle started to give out.

I struggled through intermittent rain and snow, always downward, to reach Cheyenne, Wyoming. If you have to break down on the road, I couldn't imagine a more beautiful section of the country to spend some unexpected time in than Cheyenne.

Almost every city has a cycle shop or one close by and Cheyenne was no exception. In short order the bike was repaired and I received instructions on how to get through the pass at Ogden, Utah, before an approaching storm headed our way.

I thought I'd play it safe, waiting out the bad weather in Rock Springs, and continuing on the next morning. As I set out, I had no idea that the storm had slowed, and bad weather was awaiting me at the pass.

It started to rain heavily; then worse yet, the rain turned to snow. The snow caked my helmet shield, cutting my view of the road ahead, so I rode slowly up the parking lane at the side of the Interstate. Trucks and cars ahead of me were beginning to pull over. This was no snow flurry, it was a spring blizzard.

My hands and feet were already numb with cold. I longed for the comforts of a city . . . any city. Like the pioneers of old, it seemed I was to have my endurance and perseverance tested in this passage across the Rockies.

I crept over the mountain pass, into a little town called Brigham City. As I stood at the registration desk of a motel, dripping snow and ice from my rain suit, the owner told me with a warm smile that she wouldn't have turned me away even if I didn't have a dime.

Cold and miserable as I was, I could still say the rewards of the trip had far outbalanced the hardships.

Brigham City is near Promontory Point, where the golden spike joined railroads from east and west into the first cross-country line. Even today, the West would be hard pressed to survive without the links to the rest of the country provided by rail and truck lines. Railroad workers and truckers are the modern-day Western adventurers.

Engrossed as I was in the scenery, I didn't notice a small creature about to cross the highway. As I passed, it skittered back into the woods, but not before leaving its scent behind.

Stopping for gas at the next station, I wondered why everyone backed away from me. It wasn't until I got out from under my helmet that I had began to smell the distinctive odor that had been added to my yellow rain suit.

The attendant suggested I climb out of the rain suit and hose it down with the station's disinfectant. I didn't smell a whole lot better, but at least people no longer backed away. They limited themselves to a stare that said, "she must have bugs."

By the time I reached Portland, Oregon, I had spread the scent of skunk across miles of countryside, but smelled halfway respectable myself.

I continued on to Sea Quest State Park, near Mount St. Helens. It was near dusk, too late to see any part of the mountain which had put this area on the map. The next day I rode to Toutle, where the Toutle River flows down from Mount St. Helens. Once clear and beautiful, the Toutle still

14

runs with muddy water and ash, one year after the volcano's destructive eruption last May 18.

Leaving the motorcycle behind, I hiked up the river in the mud, into what has been designated as the red zone. Here, the destruction left in the wake of the eruption last May was obvious. Trees had been sheared off at the ground and scattered like children's Tinker Toys by the force of the blast. A mud flow wound its way outward from the base of the volcano.

I walked to the base and stared upward to where the top was shrouded in clouds. Perhaps it was appropriate that, when I returned to camp that afternoon, I first heard about President Reagan having been shot.

Heading south after my stop at Mount St. Helens through Washington State and Oregon, it seemed I had finally left cold weather behind. But I was due for one more surprise as the cold returned just before reaching Redding, California.

It was raining and the wind was gusting to 40 knots. By the time I reached the valley, my rain suit had been ripped to shreds. Even the teeth in the zipper had been pulled loose.

A note to those traveling by motorcycle: don't try to replace a rain suit in California. The bike shops seem to subscribe to the Chamber of Commerce slogan that it never rains in that state. Needless to say, when I reached Sacramento, it was pouring.

When I finally located a replacement for the rain suit, every stitch I was wearing was soaked. Luckily, the sun came out, providing me with a natural-drying breeze.

As I rode through this California valley, both sides of the road were lined with growing things ... fields of rice and alfalfa, strawberries, groves of English walnuts and almonds, and grape vineyards. The aroma was wonderful! Water from the Sacramento and the San Joaquin deltas is pumped through the California aqueduct to these fertile valleys of the same name. It took me nearly ten hours to cover the 444 miles from Sacramento to Los Angeles, and fields of crops stretched as far as the eye could see. America at her most abundant.

In Los Angeles I had the chance to do some mechanical work on the bike. Part of the education of the trip for me was learning to do my own maintenance work on the road. Every time I stopped I always had help and with good advice and lots of help I managed.

Leaving Los Angeles for the return trip East, I crossed over Gorgina Pass outside Palm Springs. Here where the temperature was in the seventies, I passed lots of fellow motorcyclists, traveling to and from California. The desert was like a huge flowerbed, filled with every color I could imagine, spread beneath the bluest sky I had ever seen.

I made it as far as Picacho Peak State Park and called it a day. Traveling on, I discovered the desert's balancing boulders. These huge rocks, worn round by time, are piled one atop the next, looking ready to tumble in the first gust of wind. Yet they have remained exposed to the wind and the elements for eons, and will doubtless hold their precarious perch a good while longer.

The terrain was so fascinating that I forgot the tricks the desert winds can play with your gas mileage. Riding into a wind of 20 to 30 knots at 55 miles per hour will cut your mileage to one third what you might expect. I found myself miles from the next gas station in Las Cruces, New Mexico, without enough gas to reach the city.

Sure enough, a mile or so from the Las Cruces exit I was reduced to coasting. Fortunately, the city lies in a valley, and it was a downhill ride nearly all the way.

With a gas station in sight a quarter mile ahead, I started pushing the motorcycle. A man and his wife from

New Mexico State University pulled up alongside me on another motorcycle. He insisted on pushing my bike to the station, while I rode with his wife. Who says chivalry is dead?

After filling up, the three of us talked a good while. He was an assistant professor at the university and taught, on his own time, young Indians who were unable to afford a college education. This couple was willing to share whatever they had to give, including their knowledge, with those less fortunate than they. Surely they are representative of what is best in America.

Between San Antonio and my last campsite I came upon a young man beside the road repairing his bicycle. He was traveling the perimeter of the United States in order to obtain pledges for the National Epilepsy Foundation of Atlanta, Georgia. When he informed me of his intentions to visit Mount St. Helens, I told him I had just come from there and offered him one of the pumice stones I had found in the mud flow of the Toutle River. I wished him luck and we headed in different directions.

Just before reaching Gainesville, reflecting upon what I had learned about this country during my experiences and the people who share it, is beyond calculation. Each person I chanced to meet contributed in some way to helping me achieve my dream of discovering America. Perhaps, in fulfilling my dream, I gave hope to some of the dreams that each of those nameless individuals had nurtured for their own.

Traveling on a motorcycle teaches you to listen with your whole body and especially with your heart.

Total mileage: 8,178.

3
Florida to Alaska

At the top of the list was the tent, followed by pegs and hammer; crossing these out, I continued down through the list.

What appeared to be an endless job of double checking myself for the trip, was a task I enjoyed. Knowing from past experiences, that even one essential item forgotten, can be a pain if you have to hunt for that same little item in a campground store or en route.

I had gathered all of my equipment together during the last three months, anticipating the worst conditions for which all my twelve years of cycle touring experiences had prepared me.

Working as a Park Ranger in Fanning Springs, Florida, for the Department of Transportation was an advantage, mainly because part of the job is public relations oriented and from my encounters with travelers, I had gained many first-person accounts of the route from Florida through Canada connecting with the Alaskan Highway and continuing on to its end and then to Mt. McKinley, the highest mountain in North America.

Tomorrow morning seemed like an eternity as I packed my trusty 650 Four Honda motorcycle. I had soft saddlebags that fitted into wire baskets attached to either side of the bar that encircled the seat. This would prevent the gortex bags from sagging down and being burnt by the tail pipes.

I packed the small, one-burner Coleman Peak II cooking unit, along with the aluminum pot, coffee cup and other utensils on one side including enough freeze-dried food to last at least fourteen days. The freeze-dried food was great because all I had to do was add hot water and in three minutes I had a meal.

On the other side, I put the tools, flashlight, and chain lube, then in the outside compartment I placed the first aid kit and my personal items. All extra clothing except a rain suit was in the large over-the-seat compartment of the saddle bags. On top of this I strapped the tent bag and a small backpack, containing camera, film, maps, writing essentials, money and a one-quart canteen.

All of these piled on the seat behind where I was to sit, provided a nice backrest. The front fender and forks made a perfect place for the sleeping bag.

The cycle had been serviced the weekend before and equipped with new tires and cruise control. Gassed and ready to go, the bike with my weight combined with the luggage was 318 pounds . . . 18 pounds over the recommended limit. Not bad, I thought as I prepared to eat and get some sleep before leaving in the morning.

I was up and ready by seven o'clock and leaving my home just outside Bronson, Florida, with a reading of 26,726 miles on the odometer.

Smiling as I headed for Gainesville and I-75, I remembered that most everyone's reaction to my trip had been, "You're crazy! You're a forty-seven-year-old woman and traveling alone. Do you realize what can happen to you?"

The fact that eighty-five percent of my cycle touring had been solo, including a trip to Mount St. Helens, where I had seen acres of Northwood pine trees splintered like toothpicks and felt the ground tremble beneath my feet, gave me the confidence to, as they say, "Go for it."

One of my dreams had been to travel in every one of these United States and meet the people and see the places that make this country the best in the world.

The route I had mapped out would take me through seven of the eight states I lacked to fulfill my dream, leaving only Hawaii to complete the fifty states.

As soon as I got on the Interstate at Gainesville, I saw a beautiful sight . . . a bright-colored hot air balloon descending just beside the highway. It landed twenty-five yards in front of me.

As I passed, I pulled off and quickly got my camera and tried to focus. Just then I heard a loud swoosh as they opened the flaps and let out the air, collapsing the beautiful balloon on the grass beside the balloon basket. The man in the basket smiled knowingly and I just shook my head. Even if I hadn't gotten it on film, it had been a sight to remember.

The rest of the day was spent riding in and out of showers with heavy traffic up through Georgia and into Chattanooga, Tennessee to a camping area called Nickajack Dam Recreation Area. Being a part of the Tennessee Valley Authority Reservoir, with other recreation areas in Georgia, North Carolina, Mississippi, Alabama, Kentucky, and more in Tennessee, it was well-kept and offered fishing, swimming and camping and boating, and bath houses. The camp sites were around large lakes' shore and were really nice for only five dollars a night. I dined on freeze-dried vegetable beef and rice soup with cheese crackers. Nothing had tasted as good as that meal after covering 510 miles since morning.

The next morning as I rode through the mountains, I watched clouds of mist drift across the peaks as the sun arose.

In one area as I entered Kentucky, I watched eight-and-one-half miles tick off consisting of bumper-to-bumper traffic headed in the opposite direction. It seemed they had halted traffic to pave the other side and some of the large equipment had stalled and blocked both lanes going south.

Once again, I marveled at American ingenuity. I observed people in Winnebagos sunbathing on their roofs while others had set up tables and were playing cards.

In one section I passed, young people had cassette tapes at full blast and were dancing between the cars. I loved it!

Bypassing Indianapolis and heading west, I stopped at a KOA campground in Crawfordsville, Indiana for the evening. As I ate dinner, two stray cats I later named "Slim" and "Paws," came into my campsite and I shared my meal. When I set up the tent, "Paws" went inside and proceeded to stay the entire night. I already missed my two cats at home so it was a treat having feline company with me that night and the next morning.

The fragrant smell of honeysuckle brought back memories of early mornings in West Virginia as a youngster, giving me a sense of well being as I rode toward Peoria, Illinois.

Along the way, I talked with people from Nebraska. They were concerned with the state highways throughout Illinois and Indiana. On a scale of one to ten, I'd rate their roads at a four, but the farms and scenery were so beautiful I forgot about the rough roads.

The farms were laid out in quilt fashion with different crops in each square. I could only imagine how wonderful it must have looked from the air.

The first thing I did when I crossed into Wisconsin was to buy cheese in a town called Dickeyville. Freshly made sixty-forty cheese (Swiss and American mixed) was only $1.80 and the lady invited me to sample many others. This was cheese at its best. No wonder they call Wisconsin "The Dairy State."

I spent some time in Dickeyville wandering through the Sacred Grotto that was made by a man over many years from different rocks and minerals depicting the saints.

Moving on, the scenery abruptly changed from rolling hills to lakes and the trees along the highways were exact replicas of the blue spruce Christmas trees I had decorated every year, and the smell was pure Christmas to me. There were thousands of them!

I camped near Winona, Minnesota, overlooking the Mississippi River and dined on sixty-forty cheese, raisins, crackers, and root beer. Sitting there under a cottonwood tree, I could just see Huck Finn floating down the river, and I thought to myself, *It doesn't get any better than this.* During the night, I heard the foghorns of river barges just as they had sounded long ago.

The farms took on a new look as I crossed Minnesota. They became larger and the barns were the biggest I had ever seen. Some were seven to eight stories in height.

America can be proud of her people. They are so diversified and resourceful. Huge scenes had been painted on some of the barns . . . country scenes of a farmer's daily life.

There was such a variety no one could possibly take in all of them. If I had had two sets of eyes, I still would have missed so much. It made me feel welcome and feel akin to the people of Wisconsin and Minnesota.

Later I came across some BMW riders headed for the BMW Club meet at Missoula, Montana. They were all avid motorcycle enthusiasts and had traveled together many times.

They treated me as if I belonged with them. One couple was from Louisiana and the other two couples were from Vermont and Rhode Island. Their motto was, "If you like BMWs you are automatically a club member."

We shared stories, and, later that day, a campsite in Jamestown, North Dakota. They had trailer pods attached to their cycles, and when I saw the equipment they carried I had to admit they traveled in style.

They even had hair dryers to fill their air mattresses

with hot air and hot plates to cook on. Needless to say, all of us enjoyed each other's company.

At dawn, I was packed and ready to go and we said our good-byes and exchanged addresses. I had made an adjustment on the chain and added a quart of oil but since the bike had been purring along so well, I was not overly worried, so I headed for the Teddy Roosevelt National Park and hopefully a look at some buffalo.

I noticed the map indicated National Grasslands along Route 85. It was here I was to get a special treat.

As I left Interstate 94 and turned north, I saw no houses, no farms, not even fences—just grass. I hadn't been aware of the vast acres of grasslands set aside by our government.

It was still morning and I was cruising at around 50 miles an hour, when out of the corner of my eye, I saw movement. There to my right, not very far away, were deer running and leaping through the grass, maybe ten altogether with the sun gleaming on their fawn-colored fur; the tall heather grass blowing and weaving as waves. It took my breath away.

While in Teddy Roosevelt National Park, I saw my first herd of buffalo. It was hard to imagine that in the past there were herds of buffalo so vast that it took nearly a day to pass a certain point, and they covered the horizon.

There were so few cars, I could understand how wild animals remained in this protected area.

Heading west to Montana, I rode through Fort Peck Indian Reservation. Here along US 23 was the old West Trail, dotted with historic sites of many old forts.

Fort Buford and Fort Union were so close to the Canadian border that they had at one time been our only outposts in the far North. My ancestors, the Blackfoot Indians, crossed the very trail migrating north and south with the seasons along with other tribes.

Beside the highway, I saw flint rock similar to that used

by the Indians for arrowheads. There were few trees and nothing was wasted. They even mowed and bailed the grass beside the road.

In my opinion, Montana can boast of having the largest yellow grasshopper in the country. I could not encompass one of their grasshoppers in my hand. It was so large, it stuck out on either side and managed to spit juice all over my rain suit.

Most of the soil was glacier moraine, spotted with piles of large rocks every so often. The air was permeated with a smell of fresh cut hay and the landscape suited Montana's State motto, "Land of the Big Sky." I actually felt as if I could reach up and touch the sky.

As opposed to the people I had met in Wisconsin, Iowa, and Minnesota, these people were rugged and big-hearted and lived, breathed, and dreamed rodeos.

That night at Wolf Point, I stayed at the only KOA and had the best time watching the rodeo riders come into town, water their strings of horses, corral them and head for the bars in town.

In my tent during the night, I heard the music and noises of the cowboys just as it must have been since the town was established. It was as if I had stepped into the past.

The following day as I approached the Canadian border, I began to wonder what I was getting into. So far, I hadn't really thought about having no gas nor towns within a short riding distance, but soon I would literally be on my own.

I was stopped at the line by a French Canadian guard. He asked me if I had any firearms? I told him no and then I parked to the side for inspection. After getting off the cycle, I took off my helmet. He sort of smiled and commented that he hadn't expected a woman traveling alone by motorcycle.

I returned the smile and made mention of his French accent. He turned and looked at me quizzically saying, "No,

Ma'am, I live here *you* have the accent!" to which I replied, "Touché," and at that instant I once again realized, I no longer had all the rights and privileges I took for granted in the United States. From then on, I vowed not to assume anything.

The guard sent me to be interviewed in a small office upstairs. They asked for my driver's license and then asked the following questions: where I was born, what I was going to do in Canada, how much money I was bringing into the country, what credit cards I had with me, and the proposed duration of my stay in their country.

I had three hundred dollars and an American Express card, which seemed to satisfy him. He excused himself and left, taking my driver's license to verify it with computer help.

When he returned, he asked why I had three cans of oil strapped to the pile on the back of my seat. Since I had had trouble finding 20 w 50 motor oil for the cycle, I had bought three quarts before leaving the U.S. I explained this and jokingly said, "Someone had to get the oil through Canada."

He chuckled and told me to follow him, and then he actually ran down the stairs where he turned me over to another guard who did not ask me to unload anything, nor did he check further. I was on my way within five minutes.

Riding by the other visitors with their luggage open and being searched on tables, I could only surmise that because I had on a State of Florida Park Ranger Jacket and I was who I said I was, they had not questioned me longer.

They definitely knew what they were doing.

The highway over the border was four-lane and paved all the way to Calgary. What a scene it was! The land was covered with a yellow flowered plant called canola from which they make oil for cooking, baking, and frying.

Alberta's countryside is brightened every summer with the delicate flower and her economy is boosted greatly because the canola plant is grown and processed in Alberta.

Calgary was a modern city with the attitude of a boom town. It had all the big city facilities along with rodeos and a keen interest in their historic background.

I made good friends there and learned a great deal more about Canada. They are much like us except there are less of them.

The money exchange was not difficult, although our American dollar was worth more in the exchange, their prices were higher which made up for the difference.

Gas was fifty cents more per gallon and they were on the metric system but everything was written in both English and French.

It was sunny and cool and the mountains began to appear to the West. The temperatures and the altitude may have explained why the cycle and I both were consuming more of everything. The cycle was consuming more gas and oil and I was consuming more food and water.

I stopped at Fox Creek and indulged in a motel room. When the owners found out I was alone, they gave me part of their storage space for my motorcycle so I could make chain adjustments again and check everything.

The owner and his wife were fascinated with the trip I was making and the adventures I encountered. They insisted I take some of their food with me the next day and gave me the key holder to my room, number 118, as a souvenir. I would meet many more wonderful people like them before the trip was over.

At Dawson Creek, I entered British Columbia and began the Alcan Highway, which was an adventure in itself.

I couldn't believe the roads! They were made up of gravel and mud and full of potholes as deep as one half the diameter of my front wheel. There were swarms of mosquitoes that are like black clouds, and horseshoe turns, and no guard rails, and no towns, and no people for miles—but

26

most of all it was a ride in beauty unsurpassed by anything I had ever seen before except in the Grand Canyon.

I dodged rocks as big as marbles flying through the air off the truck tires of twenty-two wheelers barreling down the highway, and I had large birds swooping down in front of me. One time around a curve, I came upon a herd of wild horses and another time a porcupine. You just couldn't beat it for living life to the utmost.

There were so many cars passing me with broken windshields and broken headlights that I pulled over and taped a towel over my headlight and rags over the blinkers.

Someday they will find a pavement that will hold up to the perma frost and frost-heaves and the entire Alcan Highway will be paved, but for me, it was like sliding the big slope, running white water, and hang gliding all rolled into one and more.

The "Alcan" is a real challenge, not only by motorcycle, but by car, by camper, or even by bicycle and there were a lot of bicycles, too . . . think about it . . . during World War II in March of 1942, 10,000 service personnel and 6,000 civilians took eight months and thirteen days to complete the Alcan Highway from Dawson Creek, through the dense northwoods wilderness to Fairbanks, Alaska.

Imagine the work and hardships put into that highway. I could feel it every mile of the way.

The woods were so thick you could not see more than three feet into the trees and wild animals roamed freely across the roads. I never knew what I would find around the next curve.

It began to get colder at night, sometimes getting down to 40 degrees. Canada's camping areas were called Waysides and were just off the highway and were free. Each one offered tent sites, camper sites, extremely clean outhouse rest rooms, cut firewood, a hand pump for water, and each Wayside had one large shelter for backpackers without tents.

You had to boil the water for ten minutes, but it was, after all, usually the only water for miles.

You could purchase for ten dollars at the Welcome Stations in the cities, camping permits, good for all of Canada's Provincial Campgrounds. They were slightly better, having hook-ups and being three or four miles off the main road. Some even had showers.

There were also the commercial campgrounds near the cities for around five dollars a night and these offered all accommodations.

The gas stations were about 50 miles apart and were called lodges. Many had American brand-name gas, but the main problem was that sometimes your next gas stop would be closed and out of business, so I had to keep at least 1/2 tank of gas if possible.

You could rate the lodges by how many different mounted animal heads they had on the walls. The more heads, the longer they had been in business.

The lodges were log homes with the front built into a restaurant and gift shop. In the back was a building housing the diesel or gas engine that ran the generator twenty-four hours a day for electricity. That's right, no electricity outside the cities.

The owners were real pioneers and great story tellers. It was fun to stop and hear about how they lived and hunted those northwoods.

I met a lady named Ida and her two teenagers, Kim and Andy, at a lodge near Whitehorse in the Yukon. They were from Fairbanks and we had breakfast together and I learned more about Mt. McKinley and the National Park. Ida and her family were fun to be with and knowledgeable about the area. We chatted for quite a spell.

The chain on the cycle gave out. No more adjustments. I would have to find a motorcycle shop and the next town was Whitehorse, so I decided to stop in a commercial campground which would enable me to have a shower and wash some clothes.

I had mud an inch think on me and on the cycle. Since it was Sunday, I would have to wait till Monday to get a chain so it gave me a chance to look around Whitehorse too.

I stopped at a place called Sourdough Campground and started unpacking and cleaning everything. Later I rode into Whitehorse to a paddle-wheeler that used to cruise up and down the Yukon River during the gold rush era. They had grounded it and made a museum on board. It reminded me of the Delta Queen paddleboat I had been on in the Mississippi River a few years back.

Just outside town I saw Ida and her family again. They had stopped at an information booth and small park area. I was amazed at the amount of things we had in common. I said I would try to visit them in Fairbanks if I possibly could, and we exchanged phone numbers before we parted again.

When I returned to the Sourdough Campground, I noticed a young woman and an older lady sitting on a bench near me. I smiled and said, "Hello." They asked where I was from and where I was headed.

When they found out I was from so far away, they asked if I would like to visit that evening with their family at their home.

The woman's name was Sandy and she and her father-in-law came to pick me up that evening. They lived about five miles away in a cabin she and her husband, Jim, were building. Jim's mother and dad were visiting from Toronto.

Sandy was from South Africa and Jim had been born in Canada. His parents were from Ireland, originally. The father had served in Africa under General Montgomery during World War II. He had fought against the Africa Corps and General Rommel while riding motorcycles, mounted with machine guns, in the desert.

We had dinner and I sat there in pure ecstasy, listening to the father tell of fighting in Alexandria and Tobruk and seeing General Rommel.

The evening was over too soon. I explained that I had to get up early to try to find a chain for the cycle, and Jim kindly offered to help in any way he could if I ran into any trouble getting parts the next day. I found this attitude, typically, a national trait, the willingness to offer help to travelers.

When I was back in my tent, I laid there thinking about all the history Jim and Sandy's small son, Michael John, would inherit from being born into that family. Just amazing!

I was at the Honda dealer's door at opening time. They were happy to help me and fixed the bike with a new chain and checked everything out. They wished me a safe journey and I was on my way by ten-thirty.

I met some more fellow Americans at my next campground. They were on their way to Anchorage. By this time, I had crossed so many time zones, I had no idea of the time of day. I had noticed that I felt awfully tired and that daylight lasted longer.

I found that I was falling asleep in my tent before dark every evening. When I finally asked the time and set my watch, I was astonished. I had been traveling sometimes till eleven P.M. and then camping for what I thought was about seven or eight hours, when it had, in fact, been only four hours or less.

I was informed that it does not get dark up there. At about two-thirty A.M. it appears as dusk for maybe an hour and then it is daylight again. Three months of the year there is no darkness and for some time in the winter there is no daylight up there. No wonder I had been so tired.

The next time I stopped to camp I slept a full eight hours.

Passing through customs once more, I had that old feeling I always get upon reentering the U.S. I felt safe and confident of my rights as an American citizen again.

I went through a town called the North Pole and then Fairbanks, Alaska, before I saw the sign DANALI NATIONAL PARK, 115 MILES.

The park's name had been changed from Mt. McKinley to Danali in 1980 when they expanded the park to include four million more acres, making a total six million acres of the land in the park; "Danali" being the native word for the "high one," the massive peak we know as Mt. McKinley.

Arriving at the park, I went to the information center first, but all the campgrounds at the park were full. The rangers told me it was always first come, first served. They said to try the campgrounds outside the park.

There was an Airstream convention at the park so the campgrounds outside were full too. I never saw so many trailers in one place in my life. It looked like silver bumps in rows for two miles!

I saw people camping along the road so I went a little farther back and pitched my tent by the Nanana River, which was part of the boundary of the park.

I found a place with surrounding bushes which cut off the winds. It was cold—about 50 degrees. The river was fast and ran through a canyon.

As I sat there, I could see the top of Mt. McKinley and the rapids in the river. It was a magnificent sight.

Private outfitters offered raft trips down the river and the park offered free bus trips on a shuttle basis and of course there was backpacking.

They had an eight-hour bus trip which I decided to take advantage of the next day. I was able to see Dall sheep on the ridges and a brown bear with her cubs, and red fox and arctic ground squirrels. You could leave the bus at any time to go backpacking except when animals were sighted. That was for their protection as well as yours.

I backpacked one day and saw more wild life in that one day than I had seen in the last twenty years.

There must have been one thousand different shades of green around me, and every kind of rock imaginable lying on the ground, washed down from the mountains.

I loved it. It was as it had been in the beginning with only nature to change it.

The last evening before heading home, I sat in front of my tent and marveled at what I had seen and learned on this trip. The majority of people outside the Alaskan cities are pioneers. Alaska is the last true wilderness America has to offer. Our government is trying to keep the major part of this vast and beautiful state as nature intended it . . . it's cold, it's hot, it's rugged . . . it's what the rest of America used to be like before it was populated.

The biggest moose in the world is there and the biggest bear, the brown bear, in the world is also there. I didn't know at that time that my near miss encounter with a brown bear on the way home would keep me in Alaska longer than I had planned, but that is another story altogether.

At that moment I was thinking only of the beauty surrounding me and that every American should have a chance to make the trip up the Alcan Highway to Alaska, giving up our modern conveniences for awhile and struggling through the northwoods. Maybe then, they would be able to sense and feel some of the wonderment that our ancestors must have perceived, just as I had on this trip.

Packed and ready to go.

Typical state park campsite.

One of my favorite places, Picacho State Park, Arizona.

Mount Rushmore, part of the American heritage, South Dakota.

One of the many roadside faith grottos, Mexico.

An awesome background, the Grand Canyon, Arizona.

My first sight of real buffalo, Yellowstone Park, Wyoming.

The bright yellow canola plant so prominent in Canada.

At the border of Alaska.

The highest mountain in North America, Mount Danali.

Caught in a snow storm, Utah.

Part of the devastation below the crown of Mount St. Helens.

Along the Alcan Highway the old Yukon Paddle Boat, Canada.

4

Into Mexico and Back

The woman was saying, "You just can't ride down into Mexico alone on a motorcycle, it just isn't done."

That was the warning I received when I stopped at the El Paso tourist center on my way to the border at Nogales, Arizona.

I had explained my intentions of traveling down Mexico's West Coast to Mazatlán and then crossing by ferry to La Paz, then up the Baja to California. The immediate result was an alarmed receptionist, desperately trying to convey her concern for my safety.

It did not deter my resolution of traveling in Mexico alone by motorcycle, but I did take heed of the warnings to stop along the highway only if no one were around and never camp near populated areas. It was good advice, I found out later.

Leaving El Paso, I rode directly to Nogales, Arizona, and spent the rest of the day getting insurance and exchanging American dollars for pesos.

Always before, I had experienced only the tourist border towns and I felt I had never really seen what the country of Mexico and its peoples were truly like.

Bright and early the next day, I packed up the motorcycle and crossed the border to Nogales, Mexico, sister city of

Nogales, Arizona, and began my journey down the west coast.

It was surprising to me that the border guards asked only why I was entering Mexico and how long I intended to stay. They checked my passport and gave me some stamped tourist papers and did not even search my luggage.

Upon leaving the border city another group of Mexican guards in khaki uniforms holding guns stopped me. They approached and began to punch the back of the motorcycle and at the same time asked for papers. They also wanted to know if I carried any guns.

I told them no and while they were examining the papers, I noticed they were searching a van with California tags. The seats were out of the van and the wheels had been removed.

They then returned my papers and motioned me on. That was the first time I had ever had a gun pointed at me by authorities and I was a little shaky as I rode south.

Determined to still see the "real" Mexico, I settled down and began to enjoy the ride and the beauty of the countryside around me.

The farther south I went, the more people I saw walking along the highway. Many were without shoes.

There were houses and huts with no doors or windows, and I could see no electrical wires anywhere.

A great deal of men—teenagers to old men—were present at all the rest stops, and the rest stops were very dirty and unsanitary. I decided to pass by and use only the facilities at gas stations.

I stopped once when I couldn't resist taking a picture of the beautiful wildflowers beside the road and then only when it was clear of people in both directions as far as I could see.

All the gas was called Pemex and my Honda 650

seemed to run just as well on it as any other gas. The money exchange gave me an advantage because our American dollar was worth 300 pesos, enabling me to pay about $1.85 for a tank of gas as compared to $4.35 in the U.S. The gas stations were always in or near a city, none along the highway or country roads.

As I came to the outskirts of Hermosillo, I was again stopped and questioned and they checked my papers, but this time, they were even less polite.

The guards searched my pack and several different men looked at my papers. They also had guns drawn. Fortunately, they decided everything was in order and allowed me to continue. Hermosillo was a large city and even though it was 125 miles from the border, I saw the difference in graffiti immediately. Compared to the normal statements found on overpasses and retaining walls, including "Juan loves Maria" and "Viva El Mexico," I now occasionally saw anti-American signs.

In the cities, I was treated with friendliness and kindness but outside the cities it was completely different. Stopping at a café along the road, I saw children playing. They were bright-eyed and happy-looking but the faces of the older people nearby showed resentment and hostility. Another change I had not seen in the border towns. It was hard to realize these were people whom I had never seen before in my life, yet, because I was an American, they resented me.

Camping on the beaches is free but can be hazardous to your health. Nevertheless, I camped on the beach and enjoyed the solitude of the Sea of Cortez. Several Spanish families traveling through Mexico by car stopped by my campsite and asked questions and stressed in all politeness that it was very foolish to travel alone being a woman and without protection.

Farther south I saw more and more evidence of vandalism and theft. Vehicles were on blocks, stripped and burned beside the roads.

I saw no police or soldiers except in the cities or at their outskirts and some of these police had no uniforms but carried guns. They always checked my papers and asked questions.

Guayamas was one of the towns I could travel by ferry to the Baja, so I spent some time finding and deciphering the information I gathered about the ferryboat crossings. It seemed that the schedule for my crossing was not for two days yet, so I decided to try my luck at Mazatlán to the south.

Just outside the city, I was stopped again, but this time by a young man who was pointing a submachine gun at my head. By now I wasn't sure what was going to happen. Another man with a rifle took my papers and disappeared behind a small adobe building. Neither guard wore a uniform.

I took off my helmet while they checked the pockets on the pack. This caused quite a stir. Understanding enough Spanish to get by, I could tell they were amazed that a woman would travel alone in Mexico. They were using the word "loco."

With gestures and words, they asked me if I felt safe traveling alone in their country. In my best high school Spanish, I told them I felt as safe there as I did on some streets in Ciudad Nueva York.

This gave them a real laugh and then they became friendly. Soon the man with the rifle returned with my papers and, with a pat on my shoulder, I was sent on my way.

Feeling very lucky, I rode away thinking about the stories I had heard of people who entered Mexico, disappeared, and were never heard from again.

I stayed in the city that night at a motel and the next day

made up my mind to forget the Baja Peninsula and hopefully make it back to the U.S.A.

It became hot and dry and the road was not paved so well now. I rode through the towns stopping only for gas and guard checks.

That night I camped near the highway but far enough away so as not to be seen from the road. Needless to say, every time I heard a car pull off the road near me I was wide awake. I got little sleep that night.

Late the next day, I crossed the border into Arizona with a great deal of relief. The U.S. Customs people were courteous but curious and did not detain me more than fifteen minutes. In fact, it was I who asked the most questions about the guns the Mexican guards had and the constant searches.

It was their contention that I was lucky not to have been robbed or worse, traveling alone as I had in Mexico. As for the guns, it seems that the Mexican authorities were trying to stop the movement of arms through their country to Central America.

I could understand the precaution they were taking but failed to see how I could have been considered as a transporter of arms, especially traveling by cycle. All the same, it felt good to be back in the U.S.A. and safe again.

The air was so clear in the desert and the sky was so blue that the shadows and colors are strikingly sharp. I decided to head for a state park I remembered in Arizona called Picacho Peak State Park, near Tucson.

One of my dreams had been to return to that park and climb the peak, so my destination became Picacho Peak.

The campsites in the park are nice and each one has a picnic table and there are showers and washrooms. The luxury of stopping in a clean place with good water and sanitary facilities is something every American citizen should be grateful for, even though there is a small fee.

My tent was pitched on sand that was heated by sunlight during the day and as I lay down that night it was as if the earth's warmth had enveloped me as the night became cool.

On the trail the next day (which took four and a half hours to reach the top and descend), the temperature was 109 degrees and I was glad I had a two quart canteen of water with me.

During the first part of the climb, when I reached a *ramada* (Spanish for shade), I rested and caught my breath. The higher I climbed the more it became a challenge but the reward upon reaching the top was worth all the struggle.

There I saw my first pair of wild peregrine falcons hunting along the crest of the peak. Then I looked out over the horizon and saw an entire train, all 183 cars stretched out across the desert floor. From my vantage point, they appeared to be the size of matchboxes.

In any direction I could see the line of sky to land. It was awesome and yet soothing at the same time. I couldn't help but wonder how many other adventurous souls had climbed the peak before me.

Not really wanting to descend to the desert, hunger forced me to do so. I spent the rest of the day changing the oil in the cycle and making a few adjustments. The 650 Nighthawk had performed well so far making my journey trouble-free mechanically. It was with a good feeling as I traveled north toward the Grand Canyon.

The towns and cities seemed so clean and friendly. It gave me joy to see a group of German tourists traveling in a van completely at ease and unafraid and laughing. I had had just the opposite experience in Mexico and realized that there are no real restrictions on traveling in the U.S.A. by foreigners if they enter through customs and leave legally.

The Canyon was as beautiful as ever and I could see hundreds of visitors tramping up and down and all around the paths. There is so much to see and do but for me the best was the hike down to the Colorado River and back up Bright Angel Trail, which is also used by the mule trippers.

It was fun just being tired at the end of the day and then sleeping on a mattress of pine needles underneath my tent at night.

I spent several days wandering and enjoying the scenery and listening to lectures given by the park rangers. You can learn so much from our State and National Park programs.

As I rode toward the east, I thought to myself about all the beauty and adventure I had crammed into two and a half weeks. Memories to enjoy and relive until my next trip.

The trip could be summed up in a western sunset so bright red and yellow I felt privileged to observe it outside a place called "Campground U.S.A."

5

Cycle America

It didn't matter that it was cloudy and rainy that morning, because my spirits were so high. I was off on a trip to Canada and across the United States by motorcycle.

Traveling by cycle these last few years has been a rewarding experience, not just seeing this great country of ours, but Mexico and Canada as well (Hawaii being the only state I've missed).

Everything was on the cycle including extra heavy clothing for Canada. Spring is cold up there; for that matter, so is summer. Guess I've gotten used to sunny Florida.

I left Delray Beach and headed north on I-95. Using the Interstate highways is the easiest and fastest way and when I want to see something special I leave the Interstate for a state or county road.

Being a woman and fifty years of age has not made me lose my love of camping and being out-of-doors, it has in fact, intensified my feelings. I'm never in a hurry and I can see so much more on the cycle. You're just a part of the landscape instead of driving through it.

I took one last look at the ocean in Juno and continued north toward my first campground in Georgia where I met another traveler, Jane Schnell, a retired government worker traveling by bicycle around the perimeter of the U.S. She had already been at it for six months.

All of a sudden, my trip seemed like an everyday occurrence after listening to her stories. That is one of the great bonuses of traveling like I do: meeting people and getting to know them.

Through South and North Carolina, I had the overwhelming sense of honeysuckle smell. I started thinking about how we connect different smells with each state.

To me, Florida will always be salt air and orange blossoms, and Georgia is rich soil and paper mills. Pinewoods and azaleas remind me of Virginia, and West Virginia is misty fresh mountain air.

It was so peaceful and pleasant cruising along through Pennsylvania's beautiful Allegheny Mountains. They wound around and through until I reached the Catskills and Adirondack Mountains of New York.

At one of the rest areas I was busy rearranging the bags on the back of the cycle when I noticed an elderly lady approaching with her cane. She looked to be seventy-five or eighty years old. She looked at me and then at the piled high motorcycle and shook her head.

I thought . . . here it comes . . . she's going to tell me how foolish I am to travel the way I did and how dangerous it is. To my surprise, she pointed her cane at the bags on the back of the cycle and asked, "How in the world did ja get all that stuff on that motorcycle?" Before I could answer she told me, "If'n I didn't need this cane, I'd jump on top of that pile and go with ya!"

We both laughed at that and then we began to talk. She was special, she had lived through so many things including many presidents and four wars. She was eighty years young, by the way, and had traveled when there were only dirt roads in most of the country. Just amazing how often we forget to draw on the history that our senior citizens have stored in their memories.

My 650 Nighthawk was purring along as I rode to upper New York State on I-87. I camped at Cumberland Bay State Park that night to the sound of waves on the Lake Champlain shores.

It must have been in the lower fifties, yet the park was filled with wind surfers in shorts taking advantage of the breeze.

Most of the young people were from the colleges nearby and it was spring and warm to them. I spent along time talking and listening to their thoughts about the world around them and of course the sounds of the "Miami Vice" theme song playing on their cassettes.

I later found a K-Mart store and purchased another sleeping bag which would prove to be a lifesaver on the trip.

The next morning I crossed the Canadian border into Quebec and was asked only if I was an American citizen and my name. Far different from my trip to Alaska up the Alcan Highway.

In my opinion, Quebec is the opposite of the other provinces in that their attitude toward Americans is indifferent and they felt they were of French descent and were not a part of Canada.

The city of Montreal was old world and quaint, but like all older cities it seemed formed by outward growth and was not planned. It was pouring rain and very cold and it's easy to get lost in Montreal—and I did!

The highways are good and mostly four to six lanes, and the Trans Canada Highway is the same. I took Route 20 to 401 and then headed toward Niagara Falls. There were plenty of service centers for gas, propane, diesel and food. Some of these centers had McDonalds and Burger Kings, making them similar to our turnpikes, but with no charge for driving the roadway.

I noticed most of their trucks have twenty-two or

twenty-six wheels instead of our regular eighteen-wheelers in the states. Can you imagine our independent truckers forced to buy twenty-two or twenty-six tires?

Entering Ontario, the people were totally different. . . . All of a sudden they spoke fluent English and French but preferred English and they seemed to be glad to have American tourists in Canada. They were courteous and friendly. What a contrast between Quebec and Ontario.

The countryside was like our own North on the U.S. side, except their camping was in provincial parks at hardly any cost—or you could stay at private campgrounds for a nominal fee.

I made my way to Niagara Falls and stayed for a tour of the Falls the next day. What a place! The flowers were everywhere and so many colors it was as a kaleidoscope. There was a monastery and also a College of Horticulture . . . with a three-year curriculum and the students were responsible for the grounds of the Canadian Niagara Falls Park. Every three to six months, the flowers were changed. The Falls itself was like seeing the Grand Canyon for the first time. It's hard to believe nature can create such wonders.

Camping along the way, mostly in state parks or KOAs, I meet a lot of people and get to know a bit about their lives and the part of the country they are from and why they are traveling. The one thing that stands out in my mind is what a privilege they feel it is to travel in the U.S. This is from both foreigners and Americans, and there are a lot of people on the move throughout America.

One of the best parts of this—or any trip—was the good feelings upon reentering the U.S. and knowing I belonged here and I was a part of this country.

Riding through the city of Buffalo and seeing the steel mills and factories and all the huge farmlands and vineyards along the Great Lakes, as compared to the Canadian side, made me realize how much this country has to offer. There's something for everyone; all you have to do is look.

Among all the beauty and natural resources we have, we sometimes forget about what makes this country so vibrant and alive . . . the people . . . our greatest resource.

I kept heading west on I-90 through the valleys of Wisconsin and Minnesota, where the contour-plowed land looked like ribbons of deep brown with green strips in between the rows. Just awesome!

I stopped for breakfast at a little restaurant called Country Kitchen, which was out on the prairie with only sky and grassy fields in all directions. Had the best breakfast I've eaten. They even served peanut butter and jelly with our toast and eggs. When I stepped outside, I looked around and half expected to see "Half-Pint," from *Little House on the Prairie* of TV fame, come running over the hill.

By the time I had reached South Dakota, the winds had picked up considerably, and I had picked up a nail in my back tire at a stop somewhere along the way and unbeknownst to me, was slowly losing air from the tire. I noticed my gas mileage had dropped off and by the time I entered the town of Chamberlain, South Dakota, I definitely knew the tire was going flat. I had spotted a motorcycle repair billboard a few miles back and hoped they would have the size tire my cycle used.

To my surprise and delight, they did and could change it for me. The mechanic was a dyed in the wool motorcycle enthusiast, so we had a great time swapping stories while he changed the tire and oil.

He advised me to camp at a place near there because a front was moving through and the winds would be getting even stronger. It was the American Creek Recreational Area, built by the Army Corps of Engineers. Actually, it was a river but it was close by and I was going to have to wire for extra money through my bank the next morning anyhow, so I decided to camp for the night.

Setting up the tent by the river was no easy feat; the winds were at 25 to 30 knots by then. I ate some peanut crackers and noticed the temperature was about 70 degrees; by 11:30 that night it dropped to 44 degrees and was pouring rain. The winds got up to 40 knots . . . my tent wasn't really made for North Pole expedition and that's exactly what it felt like.

During the night, I looked out once more and there were snow flurries. It had dropped from 70 degrees to 30 degrees in a few hours and everything was wet and cold. I was so glad I had brought the extra sleeping bag.

Having resigned myself to just plain freezing. I heard someone yelling through the wind and looked out. The campers next to me in a Winnebago were motioning for me to come over and have coffee with them in their camper.

The man and the woman were retired and on a fishing trip from New York. They were as surprised as I at the change in the weather. I remained talking with them until dawn and enjoyed every minute of it.

By now, I knew this was a major cold front and I would be there at least another day, so I hurried to find a motel if possible in the small town.

While sitting in a restaurant, discouraged at not finding a place, a couple from Norway heard me telling the waitress about my predicament. They spoke up, saying they were checking out of their room and I could have that place. I jumped at the chance.

Thanks to my bank in Florida, I had been able to have money wired to the bank in Chamberlain and I decided tomorrow would be soon enough to face the cold and rain. That night I was going to be warm and dry in my motel room.

The following day I made Mt. Rushmore by noon and climbed the stairs and path to the park building and viewing veranda. There it was, something I had dreamed of seeing since I was a child. The four faces that told respectively what this country was about: George Washington, who represented service and leadership; Thomas Jefferson, statesman and intellect; Abraham Lincoln, honesty and the right of men to be free; and Teddy Roosevelt, for his dedication to the common man and the conservation of our wildlife and lands of America for future generations.

The carving was intended to be bigger than life and the fact that Gutzon Borglum, who designed and helped carve the granite mountain, was sixty years old at the start, made me think there was hope for me yet.

Then on to the Black Hills and what a treasure they proved to be, so fascinating and somewhat mysterious at the same time. Buffalo and big-horned sheep roam at will in the Custer State Park. There were over a thousand of them and a sight to behold. I hiked back into French Creek for pictures and to see these wild animals. Camping there and being among them was such a thrill, I couldn't help but say a prayer for the people who kept the buffalo from becoming extinct. To think that at one time there were less than a thousand buffalo left on earth when in the past there were an estimated *fifty million* on the plains of North America.

A bull buffalo can be six-foot-tall at the shoulder and weigh up to a ton. What a magnificent and massive animal we almost lost forever. Watching the people as they encountered the herds in the park, I knew they too were as thankful as I.

My camera went on the blink after shooting a roll of film in the park and I was disappointed that I could not take more of the sights.

It was so wet and damp while I was there, I usually had

a hard time cooking, but once you got the crackling pine wood fire going it was warm and things like sleeping bags dried quickly. Feeling like I belonged in the Black Hills, since I had never been there before, was a sensation new to me and I enjoyed the feeling. Many presidents had frequented the park through the years and stayed in the lodges and log cabins. There is such a wealth of wildlife left to roam about the park, it reminded me of western Canada and Alaska except the roads were better.

I left Custer State Park reluctantly and took Route 87 south to Wind Cave National Park. I had never heard of Wind Cave until I saw it on the map but I won't forget it.

Upon entering, I was greeted by a small herd of mule deer. Their big rabbit ears and inquisitive eyes made them even more adorable. I came within fifty feet before they leaped away. The park offered cave tours so I took advantage of this and wandered along the cave passage ways almost 200 feet below the surface. Outside above these caves covering the rolling hills was buffalo grass that looked like rippling green velvet and interspersed amid this green was every color imaginable . . . maize, lavender, blues, rose reds; lovely wild flowers. At a distance you could see the Black Hills which were named by the Indians because the dark green Ponderosa pine grows so thickly it appears black.

Hiking into the backwoods, I came upon a pronghorn antelope . . . being curious animals (both the antelope and I), we stood there not more than fifteen feet apart and stared at each other for a full minute before he turned away. The black streak along the side of his head and the snowy white fur on his neck made a distinct marking. He leaped away as if on rubber legs, so fast I hardly had time to blink.

Clocked at 50 miles per hour, this beautiful species is second only to the cheetah of Africa.

That night I was so happy I could not sleep. To be in such a wondrous place and see these wild creatures was almost too much. I crept out of the tent and sat by the campfire and looked at the stars. They seemed so close you could almost touch them. I wished that I could give every American the chance to see all this, especially the children.

One of the featured lunches in the park concessions is buffalo burgers and buffalo stew, which I found very tasty. The sale of the over-abundant buffalo of the parks helps keep the range from being over-grazed and supports special projects in the parks.

Tomorrow I head south and east toward St. Louis but on the second night in the park, I was content to sit quietly under the swishing pines and listen to the burrowing owls calling softly to one another, "roo . . . roo" and in the distance the sorrowful sound of the native coyote.

I haven't mentioned the maintenance of the motorcycle because after you have been riding awhile it becomes second nature to you. You are so much a part of your cycle you can sense something wrong almost immediately. So, checking the oil, tires, nuts, and bolts every morning is like brushing your teeth, it is a habit.

When I have pushed myself riding a long distance, I have also pushed the motorcycle, so when I'm tired, I don't hesitate, I look for a campsite.

Riding through Nebraska was like riding in a fantasyland. All along Route 26 . . . ten feet on either side, were the most wonderful purple wildflowers called phlox. It was as a carpet and if that wasn't spectacular enough, the highway criss-crossed the Platte River and the air was literally filled with cotton fluff from the Eastern cottonwood trees growing abundantly along its banks, so much so, it appeared to be snowing.

That night I reached Kansas and tented in a KOA

Campground that was covered in clover. It was as if nature was saving the best for last, for as I peeped out the tent that night, I was treated with a light show by thousands of lightning bugs. Far to the West was the setting sun with a spectacular display of colors from light orange to pale pink and mauve to aqua.

I never saw one sunflower in Kansas, but I fell in love with Independence, Missouri, President Harry Truman's birthplace.

Stopping at the historic mansion, Whitehaven, Kentucky, was like being transported back to the Civil War era . . . from there I traveled on through Tennessee and its green rolling countryside.

When I reached I-75 and Georgia, I thought about the almost 6,000 miles and nineteen states I had covered. What a thrill it had been and I'd loved every minute, even the cold rainy weather. I knew, I too had been privileged to see some of the beauty of America.